BATHED *in* *Life*

by
Kathy Rutherford

WORD & SPIRIT
PUBLISHING
www.wordandspiritpublishing.com

Scripture quotations marked AMP are taken from the *Amplified® Bible*, copyright © 2015 by The Lockman Foundation. Used by permission. lockman.org

Scripture quotations marked AMPC are taken from the *Amplified® Bible, Classic Edition*, copyright © 1954, 1958, 1962, 1964, 1965, 1987 by The Lockman Foundation. Used by permission. lockman.org.

Scripture quotations marked KJV are taken from the *King James Version* of the Holy Bible, public domain.

Scripture references marked BARCLAY are taken from *The New Testament: A Translation by William Barclay*, copyright © 1968, 1999 by the Estate of William Barclay.

Bathed in Life

Copyright © 2024 by Kathy Rutherford
Life to You Ministries
P.O. Box 33326
Tulsa, OK 74153
lifetoyouministries@yahoo.com

ISBN: 978-1-685730-58-1

Cover Photo: Glenn Grayson (Kathy's Brother)
Text/Cover Design: Lisa Simpson,
SimpsonProductions.net

Printed in the United States of America. All rights reserved. No portion of this book may be reproduced or transmitted in any form or by any means—electronic, mechanical, photocopy, recording, scanning, or other—except for brief quotations in critical reviews or articles, without the prior written permission of the Publisher.

Contents

Introduction 5

Living in Newness of *Life* 9

Three Things to Get God's
   Life to Work for You 13

Having Victory Over
   the Enemy of *Life* 35

Scripture-Based Confessions
   on *Life* 43

A Prayer of *Life* 51

Path of *Life* Confession 53

Pro *Life* — The Gospel in the
   Light of *Life* 55

Introduction

One of the most exciting subjects to study in the Bible is the *Life* of God. Some of God's Generals who have gone on to Heaven, like John G. Lake and E.W. Kenyon, had such a revelation on this subject. I encourage you to read their books on the subject also. The more I meditate on the *Life* of God, the more I am aware of His *Life* being a part of my life.

The Holy Ghost spoke to me one day and said this:

> *Water of Life Thy Word*
> *Which saturates me whole,*
> *Does not disperse in vapor,*
> *But lingers life for my all.*

His Word lingers *Life* for my all, spirit, soul, and body. Wow! Isn't that exciting! When I study God's Word, I make sure I am conscious of this. Every time I meditate in God's Word, it is saturating and lingering in me. That's what I desire for everyone—for you to be bathed in God's *Life* on a consistent basis!

You can leave this book in many places like your car, your bathroom, beside your bed, at school or at work. Bathing in God's Word on *Life* will make you more conscious of His *Life* inside you. Then you'll want to share that *Life* with others too.

***Enjoy*!**

Water of Life,
Thy Word
Which saturates
me whole
Does not disperse
in vapor
But lingers—Life for
my all!

Living in Newness of Life

―――⟡―――

When death is all around us, we can experience *Life*! Psalm 91:5–7 shows us that plagues and calamities may surround us, but they will not come near us. That life is the *Life of God*, and that *Life* is in us.

The same kind of *Life* God has is placed within us.

> *I John 5:12 KJV*
> *He who has the Son has life.*

> *John 3:16 KJV*
> *For God so loved the world, that He gave His only begotten Son, that whosoever believeth in Him should*

*not perish but have **Everlasting Life.***

What kind of life are these scriptures talking about? What does everlasting life mean?

You might say, "I have a pretty good life."

Ask yourself, *Could there be more than what I'm experiencing?*

Define your life. Are you talking about a natural life, one that every human experiences?

Jesus came that we might have ***Life*** (*zōē*) and have it more abundantly. (*See John 10:10.*) It is why Jesus came to the earth. When He died for our sins, we died with Him; and when He was raised from the dead, we were raised up to newness of ***Life***. (*See Romans 6:4.*)

Living in Newness of Life

Romans 5:17 (KJV) says that we "reign in life by one, Jesus Christ."

We are meant to experience more than a natural life! How does this happen? The Spirit of *Life*, the Holy Spirit, came and imparted God's *Eternal Life* in us when we were born again. (*See John 3:3,7.*)

What is *Eternal Life*? In John 3:16, the original Greek calls it *aiōnios zōē*; everlasting, *Eternal, Forever life!* This is the "God kind" of *Life*, divine and abundant, that God intended for us to have before sin entered in.

Sin no longer has dominion over us, for Christ took our place and conquered sin for us. The enemy of *Life* (Satan) tries to keep us from having that eternal, abundant *Life*, but because Jesus' sacrifice released us from sin, we now have access into God's Presence with no guilt or shame of sin. We can now have a relationship with *Life* Himself, our Heavenly Father.

God created us to have fellowship with Him. We see in Genesis 3:8 that God walked in the Garden of Eden and visited Adam and Eve, but because sin had entered, they hid from God for the first time.

One day, by the Holy Spirit, God allowed me to feel what He experienced when He came to spend time with them, and they weren't there. I felt His disappointment and sadness.

What a beautiful plan God designed of redeeming us back to Him. It was a plan that took our sins away so we could have fellowship with Him again. (*See 1 John 1:3.*) We know by the Word of God in Matthew 26:39 that Jesus **had a choice** to go with God's plan. We are glad He did!

Three Things to Get God's *Life* to Work for You

How are we to get this *Life* working in us and for us? There are three things to do:

1. Meditate on God's Words of *Life*

Proverbs 4:20–22 KJV
20 *My son, attend to my words; incline thine ear unto my sayings.*

21 *Let them not depart from thine eyes; keep them in the midst of thine heart.*

22 *For they are life unto those that find them, and health to all their flesh.*

The more you find out what the Bible says about God's Word and how important it is in your life, the more you grow to love it.

Two old hymns express this well. Take note of their lyrics.

Wonderful Words of Life
by Philip Paul Bliss

*Sing them over again to me,
wonderful words of life*

*Let me more of their beauty see,
wonderful words of life*

*Words of life and beauty,
teach me faith and duty*

*Beautiful words, wonderful words,
wonderful words of life*

Three Things to Get God's Life to Work for You

*Beautiful words, wonderful words,
wonderful words of life*

Holy Bible, Book Divine
by John Burton

*Holy Bible, Book Divine,
Precious treasures thou art mine
Mine to tell me whence I came
Mine to teach me what I am.*

The writers of these hymns knew how precious and necessary the Word of God is for life. They learned to respect it as God Himself talking to them. They treasured the Bible; they ate of it; they pondered it; and they knew it was the way to have a victorious life.

They claimed God's Word as their own, and that is what we should do. We should claim it and see His Holy Words as precious treasures.

1 John 1:1–3 KJV
***1** That which was from the beginning, which we have heard, which we have seen with our eyes, which we have looked upon, and our hands have handled, of the Word of life;*

***2** (For the life was manifested, and we have seen it, and bear witness, and shew unto you that eternal life, which was with the Father, and was manifested unto us;)*

***3** That which we have seen and heard declare we unto you, that ye also may have fellowship with us: and truly our fellowship is with the Father, and with his Son Jesus Christ.*

Read 1 John 1:1 out loud to yourself. It will bless you! *That which was from the beginning, which we have heard, which we have seen with our eyes, which we have looked upon and our hands have handled, of the Word of life!*

Anyone who has heard of the wonderful words that brought you to salvation knows how precious that first verse is.

2 Corinthians 5:17 KJV
Therefore if any man be in Christ, he is a new creature: old things are passed away; behold, all things are become new.

John 3:5–7 KJV
5 *Jesus answered, Verily, verily, I say unto thee, Except a man be born of water and of the Spirit, he cannot enter into the kingdom of God.*

6 *That which is born of the flesh is flesh; and that which is born of the Spirit is spirit.*

7 *Marvel not that I said unto thee, Ye must be born again.*

However the Gospel message comes to you, when you personally receive what Christ has done for you and are born again, you become a "new creature" in Christ according to 2 Corinthians 5:17 (KJV), your eyes will be opened to a whole new world of eternal things!

You will see how beautiful the Word of God is. The revelation that comes as you meditate on God's precious words of *Life* will bring *Life* to you!

2. Yield to the Spirit of *Life*

John 14:26 KJV
But the Comforter, which is the Holy Ghost, whom the Father will send in my name, he shall teach you all things, and bring all things to your remembrance, whatsoever I have said unto you.

Three Things to Get God's Life to Work for You

John 16:7 KJV
Nevertheless I tell you the truth; It is expedient for you that I go away: for if I go not away, the Comforter will not come unto you; but if I depart, I will send him unto you.

The Holy Ghost (or Holy Spirit—God's Spirit of *Life!*) is the main ingredient for experiencing the life God wants you to have.

The Holy Ghost has been my encourager, my helper, and my standby. He doesn't give up on me. He believes in me. He is my partner in life and ministry.

Jesus looked to the time when the Holy Ghost could come down and indwell each one of us. Jesus could not do this because He had come as a man and could only be one place at a time.

Acts 1:8 KJV
But ye shall receive power, after that the Holy Ghost is come upon you; and ye shall be witnesses unto me both in Jerusalem, and in all Judea, and in Samaria, and unto the uttermost part of the earth.

In this Church Age[1], the Holy Ghost was to be in each one of us. It's important that we get to know Him and learn to be led by Him so we can grow and accomplish our purpose. We are the Body of Christ here on the earth.

Ephesians 1:22–23 KJV
22 And hath put all things under his feet, and gave him to be the head over all things to the church,

23 Which is his body, the fulness of him that filleth all in all.

---

[1] For further study, I recommend the book *Ages and Dispensations* by Frank Boyd or using the key words *Church Ages and Dispensations* with online searches.]

We are to know who we are and have a great understanding of our part as the body of Christ. Going forth speaking His Word is a part of it.

Praying in a heavenly language called tongues is also a vital part of having the Holy Ghost on the inside.

Acts 2:4 KJV
And they were all filled with the Holy Ghost and began to speak with other tongues as the Spirit gave them utterance.

I remember sitting in my living room as a 20-year-old wanting to say things to God but not knowing what to say. I sensed my heart wanted to empty out to Him with words, but I couldn't come up with any. I could feel it rising from within but didn't know how to release it in words.

Within a year I discovered the baptism of the Holy Ghost and speaking in tongues. I found out that God had a love language that I could speak to Him even though I didn't know what I was saying, but it gave me an utterance so I could empty out my heart to Him. I loved Him so much and wanted Him to know.

1 Corinthians 14:14–15 KJV

14 *For if I pray in an unknown tongue, my spirit prayeth, but my understanding is unfruitful.*

15 *What is it then? I will pray with the spirit, and I will pray with the understanding also: I will sing with the spirit, and I will sing with the understanding also.*

Later in that passage, verse 17 tells me that I give thanks well when I pray and sing in the Spirit.

Jude 1:20 KJV
But you beloved, build yourself up in your most holy faith, praying in the Holy Ghost.

This is another benefit of praying in the Holy Ghost. It keeps you refreshed and ready to cooperate with Him to accomplish your assignment.

3. Confess the Word of *Life*

John 1:1–4 KJV
1 *In the beginning was the Word, and the Word was with God, and the Word was God.*

2 *The same was in the beginning with God.*

3 *All things were made by him; and without him was not any thing made that was made.*

4 *In him was life; and the life was the light of men.*

1 John 5:11–13 KJV
11 *And this is the record, that God hath given to us eternal life, and this life is in his Son.*

12 *He that hath the Son hath life; and he that hath not the Son of God hath not life.*

13 *These things have I written unto you that believe on the name of the Son of God; that ye may know that ye have eternal life, and that ye may believe on the name of the Son of God.*

You become His very own child, born of God according to 1 John 3:1. His divine ***Life*** produced ***Life*** in you. Now with "***Life*** Himself" on the inside, you can speak and have God's ***Life*** manifest in you and for others.

We are like Him. God brought forth Jesus, the Word of *Life*, by the dynamics of words. In creation, God spoke, and with His words, He created this world we now enjoy. (*See Genesis 1:1–31.*)

I was fascinated when I read Hebrews 1:3 where it said, "upholding all things by the word of His power." I saw that Jesus had all power, but that power wasn't released until words were spoken!

Psalm 33:6 KJV
By the word of the Lord were the heavens made; and all the host of them by the breath of his mouth.

Psalm 33:9 KJV
For he spake, and it was done; he commanded, and it stood fast.

Using Our Mouths to Produce *Life*

Proverbs 10:11 KJV
The mouth of a righteous man is a well of life.

Proverbs 15:4 AMP
A soothing tongue [speaking words that build up and encourage] is a tree of life.

Our mouths should be used to bring forth ***Life***!

There are three incidents here God showed me how negative words brought negative results, and I want to share them with you.

The first incident was after I heard the wonderful Gospel preached at the age of 12 and accepted Jesus as my Savior. One day, I walked to the store, and a dog followed me. It wouldn't leave me alone! I said to the dog, "I wish you would go out in the street and get hit by a car!"

As soon as the words were out of my mouth, the dog ran out in the street and got hit by a car! He ran into a bush and hid. I cried and told the dog that I was sorry for saying that.

I never forgot it! Death and *Life* are in the power of my tongue!

Another incident was when I was riding in our car and saw two women walking together on the sidewalk having a conversation. I saw into the spirit realm and noticed a dark cloud over them. The Spirit of God spoke and said, "They were talking up a storm." They were speaking negatively about something and causing a storm to come into their lives.

The last incident is a time when my prayer partner and I were together to pray and had been talking about our husbands. When we began to pray, my prayer partner saw a vision of us behind a rock throwing stones at our husbands. We were talking negatively about them instead of praying for them and speaking positive words concerning them. Words of ***Life*** were not coming out of our mouths for our husbands; we were stoning them with negative words instead.

The Lord says that the words He speaks are spirit and life. (*See John 6:63.*) Our words should be the same.

Sometimes we need help to know when our mouths are not lining up with what God's Word says. The Holy Ghost is here within us to help us. Let Him know that you want Him to help you say the right things.

Ephesians 5:1 KJV
Be ye therefore followers of God, as dear children.

The Greek word translated *followers* means to mimic or to imitate. We are to act like our Father. If we have accepted Jesus as our Savior, the Bible tells us we are to imitate our Heavenly Father. It's so fun to see children in the natural imitate their daddy's ways. I am sure the Father God likes it when we imitate Him.

Learn About God's Kingdom and His Laws

Romans 5:17 KJV
For if by one man's offence death reigned by one; much more they which receive abundance of grace and of the gift of righteousness shall reign in life by one, Jesus Christ.

The Greek word translated *reign* in the passage above means to have a foundation of power or to rule. A king declares and it is established.

Having a good understanding of how a kingdom operates helps you understand your authority you are supposed to be using. We Americans are not aware of kingdoms like people in the eastern world are. I was always attracted to movies about kings and kingdoms. It helped me visualize how I need to function in God's Kingdom.

Kingdoms operate in a certain way with laws that govern them. Just as the natural world has laws of gravity, motion, and electricity that we learn to use, so the Kingdom of God has laws that will always work if we work with them.

For you to get the laws of God's Kingdom to work for you, you must use the laws the way they were set up to work. When you learn how to operate God's laws, you will enjoy the benefits of them.

Mark 11:23 KJV
For verily I say unto you, That whosoever shall say unto this mountain, Be thou removed, and be thou cast into the sea; and shall not doubt in his heart, but shall believe that those things which he saith shall come to pass; he shall have whatsoever he saith.

This is a law in God's Kingdom: "whosoever shall say..."

You might say, "I don't want to say things, I like to be silent." Well if that's the case, you won't benefit from that law. It's your choice.

Activate God's Word for Your Life by Speaking

2 Corinthians 4:13 KJV
We, having the same spirit of faith, according as it is written, I believed, and therefore I have spoken, we also believe and therefore speak.

Let's look at Mark 11:23 again. Notice how many times it uses the words *say* and *saith*.

Mark 11:23 KJV
For verily I say unto you, That whosoever shall say unto this mountain, Be thou removed, and be thou cast into the sea; and shall not doubt in his heart, but shall believe that those things which he saith shall come to pass; he shall have whatsoever he saith.

In this scripture, you can see that *saying* is said more than the word *believing*. So, saying is a vital part of a Christians life!

What Are You Saying?

I was in my living room one day and thinking on Mark 11:23, and the Spirit of God said to me, *"What are you saying?"*

I thought about it and realized I wasn't saying anything! Actually, I was speaking my circumstances, which wasn't going to change my life to a better one. I needed to speak what I desired.

That's the Kingdom principle that will work for us if we apply it by saying out loud—not what our circumstances are saying, but what God's Word says that belong to us. There is creative power in His Word, and we must take it and say it with our mouths for it to produce the results that we want.

Saying nothing will produce nothing in our lives.

God's Word is still as powerful today as it was when He first spoke it. It's like a seed. There is *Life* in the seed, but it won't produce without planting it in the ground.

Check up on yourself and see what you are saying. If you aren't saying anything, change it and begin to speak. If you realized you are speaking negatively, repent over those negative words and begin to speak *Life* words in their place.

Having Victory Over the Enemy of Life

Jesus is our example. He spoke the Word of God to His enemy and gained the victory. Matthew Chapter 4 gives us a pattern to follow:

Matthew 4:1–11 KJV
***1** Then was Jesus led up of the Spirit into the wilderness to be tempted of the devil.*

***2** And when he had fasted forty days and forty nights, he was afterward an hungred.*

***3** And when the tempter came to him, he said, If thou be the Son of*

God, command that these stones be made bread.

4 *But he answered and said, It is written, Man shall not live by bread alone, but by every word that proceedeth out of the mouth of God.*

5 *Then the devil taketh him up into the holy city, and setteth him on a pinnacle of the temple,*

6 *And saith unto him, If thou be the Son of God, cast thyself down: for it is written, He shall give his angels charge concerning thee: and in their hands they shall bear thee up, lest at any time thou dash thy foot against a stone.*

7 *Jesus said unto him, It is written again, Thou shalt not tempt the Lord thy God.*

8 *Again, the devil taketh him up into an exceeding high mountain,* *and sheweth him all the kingdoms of the world, and the glory of them;*

9 *And saith unto him, All these things will I give thee, if thou wilt fall down and worship me.*

10 *Then saith Jesus unto him, Get thee hence, Satan: for it is written, Thou shalt worship the Lord thy God, and him only shalt thou serve.*

11 *Then the devil leaveth him, and, behold, angels came and ministered unto him.*

For us to have victory over the enemy of ***Life***, we must speak the Word of God to him ***with our mouths***.

This reminds me of an incident while going to Bible school. My husband, Tom, and I both went for one year in 1976.

After classes one day I was at home praying concerning our bills. The Lord had me get all of them and pile them on the table. We did not have the money to pay them.

My spirit rose on the inside of me, and I knew that it was not God that we were late on these bills. I seriously went after it in the Spirit. I came against the enemy full force.

A song came to me that had a line in it that said, "It is done!" I kept singing that line over and over.

I began to sing and saw into the spirit realm. A medium-size devil came up to me, and I sang, "It is done!" and he rolled backwards. He got up and came to me again. I sang, "It is done!" Once again, he rolled backwards. The third time he ran up to me, I sang, he rolled backwards, and then he left.

I knew it was done! In just a few days, a significant check arrived in the mail from someone we did not know well. It was the amount that we needed to pay all our bills. Glory! Hallelujah!

Always remember to speak the Word in your circumstances. It's where the power of God is, but you must speak it out of your mouth.

One time, a minister spoke a prophecy where the Lord was telling us that His greatest desire for His people was to have a better life by the spoken Word—that His Word has not lost its power; it is still equally as powerful today.

So let's benefit from the spoken Word and live more victorious lives!

We must speak it in faith. If you feel you don't have faith to speak it, then spend time building your faith by meditating on His Word.

Romans 10:17 KJV
So then faith cometh by hearing, and hearing by the word of God.

I can tell you if you meditate on these ***Life*** scriptures, faith will rise in you to come against death in any form.

John 10:10 KJV
The thief cometh not, but for to steal, and to kill, and to destroy. I am come that they might have life, and that they might have it more abundantly.

The devil represents death. Jesus represents ***Life*** in abundance!

If you have been diagnosed with cancer or any incurable disease, I understand that you have thoughts coming to your mind about death. (I did too.) This is the time to invade your mind with words of **_Life_** from God's Word.

John 6:63 KJV
It is the Spirit that quickeneth; the flesh profiteth nothing; the words that I speak unto you, they are spirit and they are Life.

Hebrews 4:12 KJV
For the Word of God is quick, and powerful, and sharper than any twoedged sword, piercing even to the dividing asunder of soul and spirit, and of the joints and marrow, and is a discerner of the thoughts and intents of the heart.

Bathed In Life

I was diagnosed with cancer in 2016, and confessing the Word helped me walk through it and come out victorious! If my mind was flooded with thoughts of death, I meditated on these scriptures and spoke them out loud. I was so glad I had gathered them long before I heard the words, "You have cancer!"

The scriptures in the next chapter are personalized to remind us that they are *for us*. Meditate and speak these confessions often. It will bring you from death unto **Life**! It did me!

Read them slowly. Speak them slowly. Emphasize a different part one time, and then emphasize another part or word the next time. This is how I did it, and it really ministered to me.

If I started reading without my full attention on what I was saying, I caught myself and stopped. I encourage you to do the same. Try to never be in a hurry with saying your confessions, value them. Don't take this medicine the same way you take your other medicine and vitamins; it's not a quick fix.

Scripture-Based Confessions on *Life*

I attend to your Words. I incline my ears to your sayings. I will not let them depart from my eyes. I will keep them in the midst of my heart, for they are ***Life*** and healing to all my flesh. (*Proverbs 4:20*)

I will watch over my heart with all diligence, for from it flow the springs of ***Life***. (*Proverbs 4:23 AMP*)

The words that He speaks, they are spirit and ***Life*** to me. (*John 6:63*)

Water of ***Life***, Thy Word, which saturates me whole, does not disperse in vapor but lingers—***Life*** for my all. (*Given by the Spirit*)

He is my Bread of ***Life***. (*John 6:35*)

I will not forget His law or teaching; my heart will keep His commandments, for length of days and a long life experiencing His ***Life***, and peace (harmony, wholeness, prosperity, completeness, welfare, and tranquility) shall they add to me. (*Proverbs 3:1–2*)

You have made known to me the ways of ***Life***; you will fill me, infusing my soul, with joy with Your presence. (*Acts 2:28 AMP*)

You will make known to me the path of ***Life***; in Your Presence is fulness of joy; at Your right hand, pleasures forevermore. (*Psalm 16:11*)

Scripture-Based Confessions on Life

I heard His Word and believed that God sent Jesus therefore I have ***Everlasting Life*** and will not come unto judgement. I have passed from death unto ***Life***. (*John 5:24*)

God set before me ***Life*** and death and He said for me to choose ***Life***, so I chose ***Life*** that me and my seed would live. (*Deuteronomy 30:19*)

He is the way in my life, He is the truth in my life, and He is my ***Life***. (*John 14:6*)

And this is the record, that God has given me ***Eternal Life*** and this ***Life*** is in His Son, I have His Son, so I have ***Life***. (*1 John 5:11–12*)

For if while I was an enemy, I was reconciled to God through the death of His Son, it is much more certain, now that I am reconciled, that I shall be saved (daily delivered from sin's dominion) through His **_Resurrection Life_** within me. (*Romans 5:10 AMP*)

I know I have passed from death unto **_Life_** because I love people. (*1 John 3:14*)

For the wages that sin pays are death, but I have received the bountiful free gift of God which is **_Eternal Life_** through (in union with) Jesus Christ my Lord. (*Romans 6:23 AMP*)

In Him was **_Life,_** and the **_Life_** was the light of my life. (*John 1:4*)

He is the Resurrection and the **_Life_** in my life. (*John 11:25*)

He is the vine; I am the branch. The life of the branch gets its **_Life_** source from the vine therefore the source of my life is Him who is **_Life_**. (*John 15:5*)

Scripture-Based Confessions on Life

I have received the abundance of grace and the gift of righteousness, so I reign in *__Life__* by one, Jesus Christ. (*Romans 5:17*)

Greater is He (*__Life__*) that is in me than he (death) that's in the world. (*1 John 4:4*)

God has provided for me everything that pertains to *__Life__* and godliness. (*2 Peter 1:3*)

For to be carnally minded is death, but I am spiritually minded therefore I have *__Life__* and peace. (*Romans 8:6*)

I am complete in this life for I am complete in Him who is *__Life__*. (*Colossians 2:10*)

In Him, *__Life__*, I live and move and have my being. (*Acts 17:28*)

In His Kingdom there is *__Life__* and no death, and I have been translated into His

Kingdom through His Son therefore I have ***Life***. (*Colossians 1:13*)

I've been delivered from the dominion of death into the dominion of ***Life*** through Christ; therefore, ***Life*** is dominating me. (*Romans 6:9*)

Jesus came that I might have ***Life*** and have it more abundantly. (*John 10:10*)

If the Spirit of ***Life*** that raised Jesus from the dead lives in me, He will give ***Life*** to my mortal body. (*Romans 8:11 AMP*)

The law of the Spirit of ***Life*** in Christ Jesus has made me free from the law of sin and death. (*Romans 8:2*)

I have been placed into ***Life*** for my life is hid in Christ, who is ***Life***. (*Colossians 3:3*)

With long *Life* will He satisfy me and show me His salvation. (*Psalm 91:16*)

Now I serve under obedience to the promptings of the Spirit in newness of *Life*. (*Romans 7:6*)

Christ (*Life*) in me the hope of Glory (God's manifested *Life*). (*Colossians 1:27*)

The water that He gave me is in me a well of water springing up into everlasting *Life*. (*John 4:14*)

He will give to me because I am thirsty, of the fountain of the water of *Life* freely. (*Revelations 21:6*)

Jesus Christ has abolished death and brought *Life* and immortality to light through the Gospel for me. (*2 Timothy 1:10*)

I will fight the good fight of faith and lay hold of **_Eternal Life_** and all it represents. (*1 Timothy 6:12*)

If then I have been raised with Christ, my heart must be set on the great realities of that Heavenly sphere, where Christ is seated at the right hand of God. My constant concern must be with the Heavenly realities, not with worldly trivialities, For I have died to this world and now I have entered with Christ into the secret **_Life_** of God. When Christ, who is my **_Life_**, comes again for all the world to see, then all the world will see that I too share His Glory. (*Colossians 3:1–4 BARCLAY*)

A Prayer of Life

Heavenly Father,

I thank You, first, for giving me life, life on this Earth. You have created me in Your image, and You are full of ***Life***. The real me is full of ***Life***, a ***Life***-giving substance created for You.

I understand from Your Word that we have an enemy to ***Life*** who tries to keep me from enjoying the fullness of this ***Life*** that You so freely gave me. But Jesus, the light of ***Life***, came and destroyed the power of death over me that kept me from experiencing all the ***Life*** You had given me. Now by faith, I can walk in the abundance of ***Life*** that You want me to experience.

Father, I thank You for my body that You have given me. Thank You for the privilege of walking on this earth in newness of spiritual *Life*, experiencing Your *Life* in my spirit, soul, and body.

I thank You for the indwelling of the Holy Spirit, who helps illuminate my mind to understand this *Life* You have given me. Thank You, Father, that the Spirit of *Life* also quickens my body and makes it alive.

Jesus came that I might have *Life* and have it more abundantly, to the fullest.

Thank You that the Gospel of *Life* came to me! I open myself up to You, the wonderful Giver of *Life*, and Your Son, who is the Head of the Church, that I might express that *Life* to others. I also open myself up to the working of the Holy Spirit to do as He pleases that I will be the vessel of ***Life*** to the world.

In Jesus' mighty Name!

Path of Life Confession

My steps are steps of *Life*.
I am led by the Spirit of *Life*.
I am living in the law of *Life*.
Life is dominating my path.
I walk this path of *Life* by Love.
Love is dominating my
every step of *Life*.

Pro *Life*
The Gospel in the Light of *Life*

In the beginning was God, *Life* Himself. *Life* wanted to produce *Life*. God produced Jesus.

Have you ever wondered how Jesus came about? Well, this is how. Scientists have found out that any living organism produces after its own kind. *Life* will produce more *Life*.

The creativity of *Life* began to flow in God, and God said to Jesus, "Let's make another kind of *Life*!" And God made man. God made them male and female.

Then God told them to produce *Life* after their own kind.

Life is an expression of God. Being born into this world is an expression of *Life*, which is an expression of God Himself. Can you see now why the enemy of *Life*, satan, doesn't want abortions to stop? Can you see the truth about occults that represent death, killing, and sacrificing of *Life*? The enemy of *Life* tries to get you to hate yourself and harm yourself because you are an expression of *Life* Himself: God.

Satan hates you because he hates God. The enemy of *Life* lied to Adam and Eve. And because of their disobedience, sin came and separated us from *Life* Himself, who was our source of *Life.* The enemy of *Life* thought he had won a victory, but God, the *Life* that He is, had another *Life* plan. John 1:4 says that Jesus has *Life* in Him, and that *Life* was the light of men.

He was and still is the magnification of *Life*. He became a *Life* in the form they created: man. Jesus demonstrated on the earth *Life* Himself, God, in magnification. Jesus went about doing good and bringing *Life* to all who would receive.

Then He gave His own *Life* for us. He had the opportunity to not go through with it, but He said, "Not my will but Thine be done." He gave His *Life* for us to have *Life* again—but in abundance. He destroyed the power of death over us, bringing us back to the source of *Life*, God Himself. Jesus brought to us a better *Life* than before causing us to be a totally new species of Life, with Jesus being the first born.

Bathed In Life

When we receive Jesus, the magnification of *Life*, into our hearts, God seals us with the Spirit of *Life*, the Holy Spirit Himself, causing us to cry out, "Abba Father." This new *Life* caused a Father relationship with *Life* Himself.

Jesus then went back into Heaven and sat down at the right hand of *Life*, God. Jesus is the High Priest of *Life*. He promised us that our bodies would one day experience immortality and that He would come back for us that we may live forever with Him. Till He comes, He has encouraged us to reign as a king in this *Life*, living in the abundance of *Life* because the magnification of *Life*, which is Jesus, did it for us. He gave His *Life* for us to reign in *Life*!

Have a happy *Life*!

You may contact Kathy at:

Life to You Ministries
Kathy Rutherford
P.O. Box 33326 | Tulsa, OK 74153

lifetoyouministries@yahoo.com

www.ingramcontent.com/pod-product-compliance
Lightning Source LLC
Chambersburg PA
CBHW072137070526
44585CB00016B/1713